NATIONAL GEOGRAPHIC

School Publishing

Plant Life

Juan Rueda

PICTURE CREDITS

Cover, 3, 4 (right below), 5 (left above and right), 6 (left), 7, 8 (above right and below), 9 (right), 10 (all), 11 (all), 13 (all), 16 (all), 17 (all), 18 (right), 19 (left below), Photolibrary.com: 1, 4 (left), 5 (left below), 6 (right), 9 (above and below), Getty Images; 8 (left), Lindsay Edwards Photography; 12 (all), 19 (left above), APL/Corbis; 13 (left), Brand X Pictures; 14 (left), Stock Image/Alamy; 15 (left), AGStockUSA, Inc/Alamy; 15 (right), Guy Holt Illustration; 18 (left), Creatas/Alamy; 19 (right), Image Source/Alamy.

Produced through the worldwide resources of the National Geographic Society, John M. Fahey, Jr., President and Chief Executive Officer; Gilbert M. Grosvenor, Chairman of the Board; Nina D. Hoffman, Executive Vice President and President, Books and Education Publishing Group.

PREPARED BY NATIONAL GEOGRAPHIC SCHOOL PUBLISHING

Steve Mico, Executive Vice President and Publisher, Children's Books and Education Publishing Group; Marianne Hiland, Editor in Chief; Lynnette Brent, Executive Editor; Michael Murphy and Barbara Wood, Senior Editors; Nicole Rouse, Editor; Bea Jackson, Design Director; David Dumo, Art Director; Shanin Glenn, Designer; Margaret Sidlosky, Illustrations Director; Matt Wascavage, Manager of Publishing Services; Sean Philpotts, Production Manager.

MANUFACTURING AND QUALITY MANAGEMENT

Christopher A. Liedel, Chief Financial Officer; Phillip L. Schlosser, Vice President; Clifton M. Brown III, Director.

BOOK DEVELOPMENT

Ibis for Kids Australia Pty Limited.

Published by the National Geographic Society
1145 17th Street, N.W.
Washington, D.C. 20036-4688

Product No. 4W1005052

ISBN-13: 978-1-4263-5048-1
ISBN-10: 1-4263-5048-1

2010 2009 2008
4 5 6 7 8 9 10 11 12 13 14 15

Printed in China

Contents

Think and Discuss ... 4

What Plants Need ... 6

How Plants Grow ... 8

Plants Have Parts ... 10

We Need Plants ... 14

Use What You Learned ... 18

Picture Glossary ... 20

4

soil

water

food

root

shoot

What do plants need to live and grow?
Why do people and animals need plants?

leaves

flower

stem

seed

What Plants Need

Plants are living things.
Plants need light, water, food, and air to survive.
Most plants need **soil**, too.

Sunlight, water, soil, food, and air help these plants grow.

How Plants Grow

Most plants grow from **seeds**.
All plants change as they grow.
These pictures show how a
corn plant grows and changes.

1. Corn seeds are
planted in soil.

2. The seeds open underground.
A **shoot** grows up from each seed.
Roots grow down from each seed.

shoot

root

6. The seeds from the
corncobs can grow
into new plants.

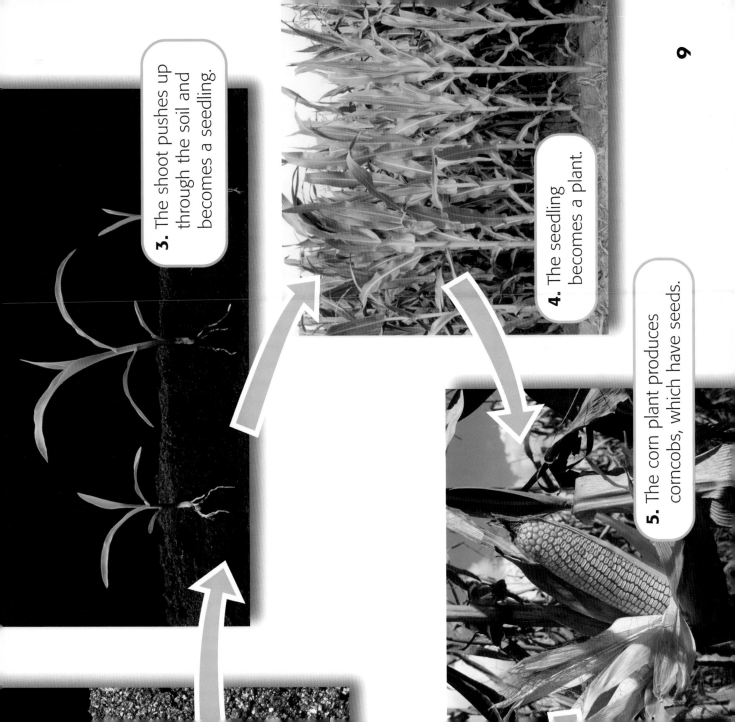

3. The shoot pushes up through the soil and becomes a seedling.

4. The seedling becomes a plant.

5. The corn plant produces corncobs, which have seeds.

Plants Have Parts

A plant has different parts.
Most plants have roots, **stems**, and **leaves**.
All the parts of a plant help the plant live and grow.

A plant's roots take in water and food to help the plant grow.

roots

Some plants have **flowers**.
Some plants have **fruit**.
Seeds can come from flowers or fruit.
Seeds can grow into new plants.

These seeds come
from a flower.

sunflower seed

peach seed

This seed comes from a fruit.

We Need Plants

People and animals need plants to survive. Plants provide food for people and animals.

People eat fruits and vegetables that come from plants.

Animals eat plants to live and grow.

Did You Know?

Plants help to produce the air we all breathe. Plants give out oxygen. Oxygen is part of the air all people and animals breathe.

Oxygen

People use plants in many ways.
Animals use plants in many ways.

People use wood from trees to build houses.

People use cotton and straw from plants to make clothing.

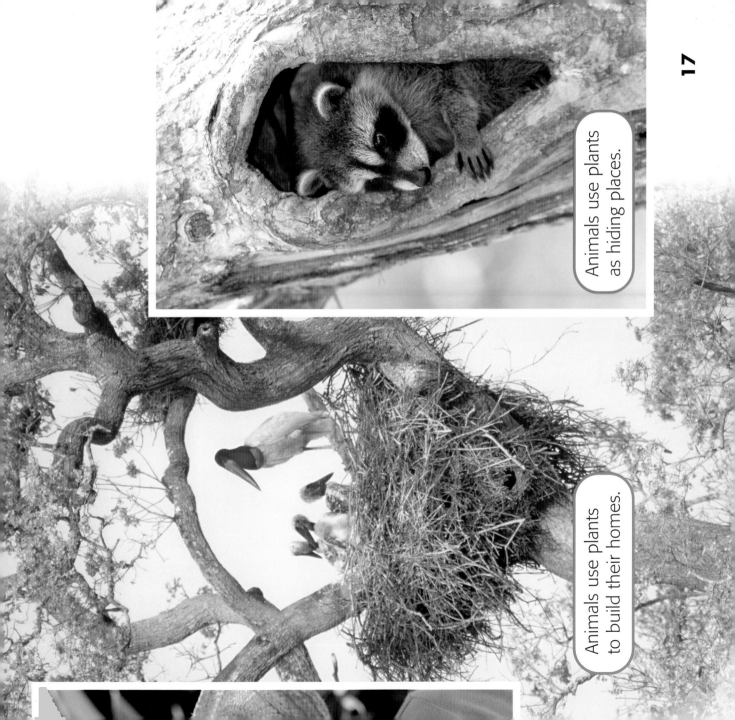

Animals use plants as hiding places.

Animals use plants to build their homes.

flowers

fruit

leaves

root

seeds

shoot

soil

stem

How do plants live and grow?
Why are plants important?

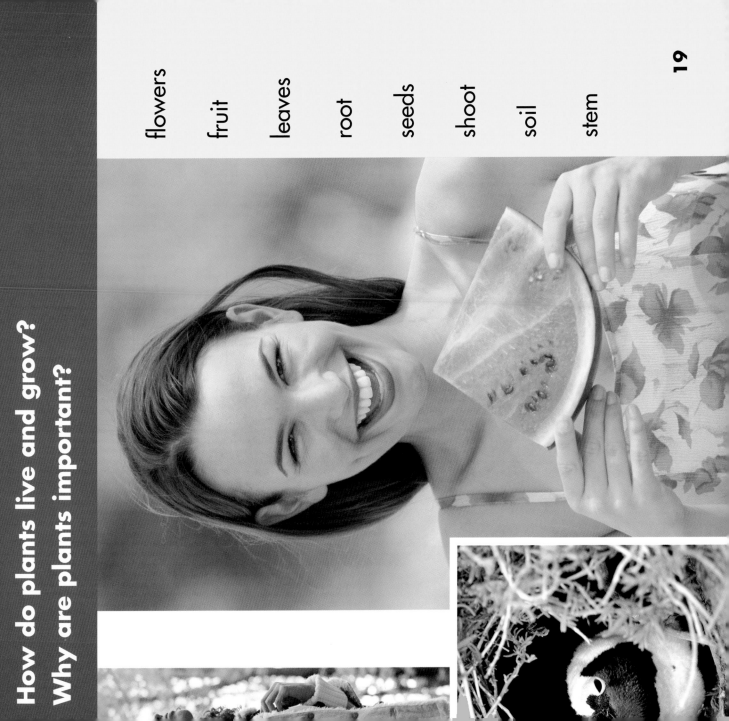

Picture Glossary

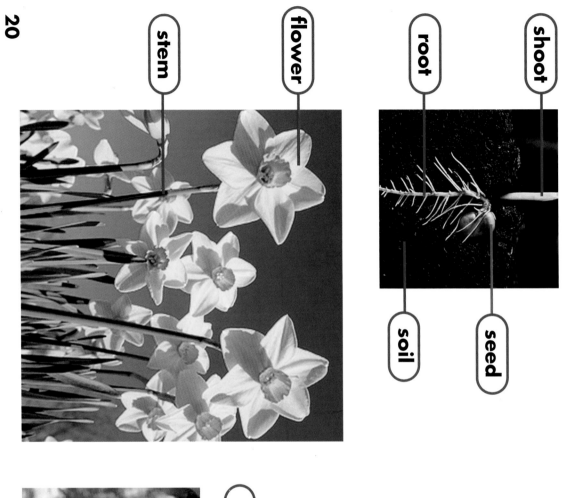

shoot

root

soil

seed

flower

stem

leaf

fruit